SHERLOCK HOLMES
THE BAKER STREET IRREGULARS

THE ADVENTURE OF THE
FAMILY REUNION

TONY LEE and DAN BOULTWOOD

First published in 2011 by
Franklin Watts
338 Euston Road
London NW1 3BH

Franklin Watts Australia
Level 17/207 Kent Street
Sydney, NSW 2000

Text © Tony Lee 2011
Illustrations © Dan Boultwood 2011
Cover design by Jonathan Hair
"The Baker Street Irregulars" logo
designed by Patrick Insole

Special thanks to Leslie S. Klinger for his invaluable contribution to this series

"Baker Street Irregulars" and the original characters
"Dr Watson", "Inspector Lestrade", "Irene Adler",
"Wiggins", "Moriarty" and "Sherlock Holmes"
the creation of Sir Arthur Conan Doyle.

A CIP catalogue record for this book
is available from the British Library

ISBN: 978 1 4451 0345 7

1 3 5 7 9 10 8 6 4 2

Printed in China

Franklin Watts is a division of Hachette Children's Books,
an Hachette UK company
www.hachette.co.uk

THE ADVENTURE OF THE
FAMILY REUNION

The story so far...

Sherlock Holmes is *missing,* believed *dead* and London has fallen into *lawlessness.*

Only the *Baker Street Irregulars,* led by Holmes's protégé Wiggins, are there to help the common people. Aided by Doctor John Watson and the enigmatic Irene Adler, the Irregulars will solve *any* crime, *any* mystery.

Three times they have fought the masked villain 'M', but Wiggins has finally seen the face of his nemesis. And while Wiggins searches for him, 'M' plans his revenge...

Wiggins   **Eliza**   **Pockets**

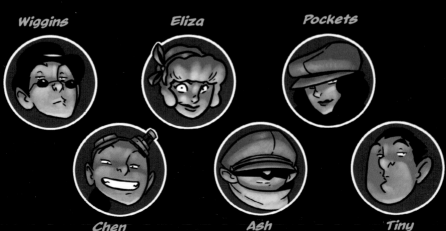

Chen   **Ash**   **Tiny**

4

A trap? All this is to *kill* me?

No, Wiggins - all this is to *hurt you.*

The *hangman's noose* will *kill* you.

Ah, *there you are* Wiggins! I wondered where you'd gone.

O'Reilly! Thank goodness you came by!

You'd *help* this boy? Even though he sent you to *prison?*

The crimes I committed with the *real* Morris Wiggins.

My *actions* brought me here.*

*See Book Three.

That can buy you a *lot* in Newgate. Like *these two* chaps, for example.

And although I'm paying for my sins, it's well known that I still received a *share of the gold.*

Military men, they are. Like me. And if you harm *one hair on this boy's head* -

- we'll *go to war on you.* Understand?

This seems to be the first time Holmes ever heard the name *Moriarty* – Morris Wiggins was *working* for him.

But surely Holmes didn't even start to *look* for Moriarty until *three years* after this?

Here are Grandfather's – I mean – *Mayhew's* notes. Lestrade gave them back to me.

Maybe Moriarty hid himself?

The Rathbone case was one of *blackmail* – but also an *insurance swindle*, it seems.

Morris was working with an *unnamed elder man* and his *son*.

"Holmes led the police to the blackmailers' hideout – and a fight commenced."

"Morris Wiggins managed to *escape* – but Holmes tracked him down."

"With Mayhew's help, Morris Wiggins was captured, arrested and taken to *Newgate* –"

"– where he was sentenced to *six years hard labour!*"

But it says nothing about a **ledger** though!

Wait - Mayhew's diary tells a **different** story!

"After **capturing** Morris Wiggins, Mayhew was **recognised** by the villain - they had **worked together**, back when Mayhew was a kidnapper."

The **mastermind** they had both worked for had a **ledger** -

- with the **payments** and **details** of all their crimes **written within!** Morris made a deal.

Find a **double** to take his place in Newgate, or Mayhew's time as a **kidnapper** would become **public knowledge!**

What did Mayhew do?

He must have **done** it - the news never came out.

But he must have changed his mind years later - **that's** why he was killed!

This ledger might even have the names of my **parents** inside!

But the ledger won't save Wiggins. His **court date** is tomorrow -

- and we haven't even found out who really killed Windibank.

15

Newgate Prison.

I know that you didn't do it, Wiggins. What I *can't* understand is why you picked up the *murder weapon.*

I didn't know that it *was* a weapon, Mister Holmes - it was lying outside the door, *handle exposed.*

By the time I picked it up and saw the *blood* - it was *too late.*

Too late indeed. They're going to *hang you* for this, Wiggins - and there's *nothing* we can do about it.

Windibank's claim of being hunted by 'Wiggins' has sealed the lid on your coffin.

But why was he even *there?* What would make him go to 221b Baker Street - where he'd *surely be arrested?*

Perhaps he was *leaving* something for you? Maybe a *note?*

If he did, it was too little, too late. My father would have *taken it* - or the police would have trampled all over it by now.

It depends where he *left it* - and whether your friends are *clever* enough to locate and *understand* it.

Because if they *can't,* Wiggins --

-- then tomorrow you will be *sentenced to death.*

And there's no way for us to *stop it.*

Yes, that's true, I suppose. I've never been sentenced to *hang*.

The benefits of working for such a great man. *Moriarty.*

All those times you thought I was him - if only you knew *how close* you were!

Moriarty ran the underworld for *decades.*

So good was he at it that even your precious *Sherlock Holmes* only discovered his identity in the *last few years.*

And I've worked for him as a trusted *lieutenant* for all of your life. I kept his *ledger*, his list of crimes.

Moriarty found a man to take my place in *Newgate*, and I moved up to a house in *Bloomsbury.*

- look where it led you.

I became the *success* that stands before you. For all your talk of *bettering* yourself, of following *Holmes* -

You should *never* have chosen to leave me for *him!*

We could have ruled *London together!*

And I *ain't* hanged yet. While we talk, my Irregulars are *stealing* your ledger. See?

Anything could happen tonight.

My boss beat *your* boss. *Remember* that, Father.

It's so nice that Joanna has found a *young man* to look after her!

She's *always* talking about you - it's *Wiggins this,* and *Wiggins that --*

Mother! Please! You're *embarrassing* me!

This is East End *accounting cant.* It's a language all of its own - like Cockney *rhyming slang.*

It's used mainly by *pawnbrokers* and *betting agents.*

So it's a *money ledger?*

No, not really - it's more for *services rendered.*

This *last* entry - it talks about *kidnapping!* These go back almost *twenty years.*

With this translated, we can pin *decades of crime* on my father.

Yes - but Windibank's murder isn't in it - which means that you'd still be *found guilty.*

If it means getting my father and his *crimes off* the streets of London -

- then I'm willing to *make that sacrifice.*

There aren't waterfalls *in* London - but there are *under* London. The *old rivers,* now covered over.

There's a man-made junction under the *Strand* where *three forgotten rivers flow into one* before reaching the Thames.

- *Reichenbach Falls!*

There's a fall of *thirty feet* before hitting the reservoir below. And the *name* local sewage workers gave it was -

Ash - find *Lestrade.* Tell him to bring backup. Tiny - take Chen and find the outlet to the Thames.

You *can't* tell *Lestrade!* If this goes wrong you'll be *arrested* and *hanged.*

And if I *don't* try, *Eliza* dies.

One way or another - *this ends today.*

'Reichenbach Falls' sewer junction.

Where is he? I said an **hour!** Is my son really so **stupid** that he couldn't work out my **clue?**

It was an easy one to work out, Father.

But then you never **were** the criminal mastermind that **Moriarty** was, were you?

Was I really that much of a **disgrace** to you?

That you felt that the only solution was to frame me for **murder?** See me **hanged?**

The murder was **accidental** – Windibank turned on me, threatened to go to the police if I didn't pay him more.

Finding him in **Baker Street** was just a **lucky break.**

You were my son. **My son!** And Holmes **took you** from me! Made you into this **fake** I see before me now.

You'll **never** be accepted by the upper classes. They'll **always** treat you like dirt!

Perhaps – but at least I wouldn't have to wear a **mask.** Or cover my face with a **scarf.** I could **hold my head up high.**

You were **always** my father – but you couldn't see that I was meant to be **more** than a criminal.

That I was destined for **greater things!**

The most haunting Horowitz Horrors are now available as superb graphic novels.